Many Christians regard me[illegible] of meditation coming from the East as suspect and at variance with the Gospel tradition. This book will set their minds at rest because the author argues that one such technique — Transcendental Meditation — is a purely natural and human exercise and is not in itself a religious practice. However, since it contributes positively to the full and harmonious development of body, mind and spirit, it is invaluable to Christians to enable them to become, as St Paul says '..mature people reaching to the very height of Christ's full stature'. *(Eph. 4:13)*

* * *

Adrian B. Smith, M.A. is a Catholic missionary priest who has been practising Transcendental Meditation since 1976 and the TM-Sidhi techniques since 1978. He is the founder of the Christian TM Group in Britain and editor and part author of *TM: an Aid to Christian Growth,* now translated into several languages.

A Key to The Kingdom of Heaven

A Christian Understanding of Transcendental Meditation

Adrian B. Smith

Temple House Books
Sussex, England

Temple House Books
is an imprint of
The Book Guild Ltd.

The Book Guild Ltd.
25 High Street,
Lewes, Sussex

First published 1993

Set in Paladium

Typesetting by Ashford Setting and Design Services,
Ashford, Middlesex

Printed in Great Britain by
Hartnolls Ltd.
Bodmin, Cornwall.

A catalogue record for this book is available
from the British Library.

ISBN 0 86332 863 6

Contents

ACKNOWLEDGEMENT

This book has been through many drafts, and each has been improved by the wise advice of friends, theologians and TM teachers, to all of whom I owe a great debt of gratitude.

INTRODUCTION

Hardly a week passes without my receiving a letter or a 'phone call, usually from a church-goer, looking for assurance that the practice of Transcendental Meditation is not in contradiction with their Christian beliefs nor harmful to their Christian living. The recent case of Jack Jones (as we shall call him) is typical.

He rang from Liverpool to say that he had been taught Transcendental Meditation a month previously and had already felt great benefit from it. In fact someone in his office had commented how well and relaxed he was looking. He answered that he had begun meditating. This conversation was overheard by a 'born again' Christian colleague who immediately warned him that what he was doing was Satanic. That in using the mantra he had been given he was unwittingly praying to Hindu gods and that if he tried to empty his mind evil spirits would enter to take possession of it.

When he 'phoned me he was really upset because the effects he had been experiencing were all so positive. He told me he was sleeping more soundly, his mind seemed to be clearer and all together he was acquiring a more positive outlook on life. Could a practice which was proving so beneficial really be as evil as his colleague had made out? Should he, as he was now being advised, give it up immediately?

I was able to assure him that there is nothing Satanic or evil about Transcendental Meditation and that as a human technique for enabling the mind to develop its unused potential, its fruits could only be of benefit to his spiritual development. To dispel his alarm I explained that there were many false ideas about Transcendental Meditation being passed around among certain sections of the Christian Church but that they originated from hearsay, from a partial knowledge and from a great deal of misunderstanding. They did not originate from Christians who had been taught to meditate and who were therefore able to speak out of their own experience.

My first draft for this present book was a series of answers to the typical questions that Christians such as Jack Jones were asking, with the object of allaying fears. But, as a friend pointed out, that would have been taking a negative approach to the subject. How much better to show this way of meditation in a positive light as it concerns our life and growth.

So this book is written mainly for the benefit of Christians who are investigating Transcendental Meditation as a possible means of improving the quality of their physical, mental or spiritual lives and are wondering how the technique relates to their beliefs and religious practice.

The Human Longing for the Divine

As far back as we can trace in human history, for centuries and even millennia before the birth of the great religions, there is evidence of a spiritual, as well as a physical and psychological, dimension in human life. There is a part of human nature that reaches beyond itself, stretching out towards the Divine, the Absolute, the Perfect.

Long before human beings arrived at an understanding that their ultimate destiny is to be in union with the Divine, the Godhead, they groped towards an experience and contact with Pure Spirit; towards an undefined 'something' which transcends the boundaries of ordinary experience.

That urge is still with us because it is a deep part of our nature. It is expressed by some through participation in one of the great religions: for others, their spiritual path lies outside structured religion.

The great religions, all of which were born less than four thousand years ago, offer an interior path of direct experience of the Divine, although for most of their adherents this way has from time to time become eclipsed by the emphasis on external ritual, morality and charitable practices.

While the great religions often name this interior path 'meditation', meditation is neither their invention nor their prerogative. As a natural, human exercise it was developed in the Orient long before any of the religions came into being.

Transcendental Meditation (TM) is a case in point. Brought to the western world by Maharishi Mahesh Yogi only within the last four decades, and now spread to all continents, it is sometimes reported by Christians as deriving from, and indeed a form of, the Hindu religion. In fact, it pre-dates Hinduism by well over 1,000 years. Its origins go back beyond recorded history to the Vedic science. This ancient eastern knowledge was a practical philosophy of life: it offered an explanation for the origin and the workings of our universe and of how humanity can live in it in a manner that is most evolutionary and beneficial.

Today many Western scientists are beginning to appreciate the value of the way the ancient East understood the world because their own findings are leading them in the same direction, particularly in the field of quantum physics. Their appreciation of Transcendental Meditation in particular arises because its benefits have been demonstrated by more than 500 scientific research studies in the fields of physiology, psychology, sociology, and ecology, conducted at more than 200 universities and research institutions in 25 countries.

As Christians, we are not locked into just one philosophical system — although our Christian theology is mostly expressed in terms of western philosophy — but we believe that Jesus is the Christ of the whole of creation and that all that is good in this world is Christ-filled.

It may seem at first sight that TM has some similarities with other forms of meditation coming to us from the East, such as Buddhist or Zen, because they are all holistic exercises designed to benefit body, mind and spirit. However, TM is fundamentally different, not only in its technique — it requires no concentration or control of the mind — but because it is grounded in the nature of all life and is no more eastern or western than the law of gravity, discovered by Newton, is a British or western law.

We can only speak of something being eastern or western when it is associated with a particular way of life, a particular culture. TM is completely independent of any life-style or culture, so it is neither eastern nor western: it is universal.

Since the transcendental state of consciousness pertains to human nature and not to religious virtue, a technique for acquiring it, such as TM, must also pertain to human nature, and in consequence be valid for all humanity of whatever culture, level of education, religious persuasion or philosophical adherence.

The Word 'Meditation'

Today, in the West, a great deal of misunderstanding is caused by the different meanings given to this word 'meditation'.

In western culture and in eastern culture the word is used quite differently. Confusion arises when we in the West understand eastern meditation in our western way.

In our part of the world before the 1960s, the word 'meditation' was used almost exclusively in a religious context. It was understood to mean a manner of praying. It is still used this way in Church circles and by writers of spiritual books, which is why many Church members have problems with forms of meditation coming to us from the East.

Religious writers and preachers in the West use the word 'meditation' to describe an exercise of the mind whereby we reflect upon some religious truth — often with the use of a text of the Bible or the words of a prayer — consciously in the presence of God. It is one way of praying. Another way of praying described in religious books in our culture is called 'the prayer of quiet' or 'contemplation'. By this is meant a state of active passivity in which no words are used or thoughts are dwelt upon, but rather it is an awareness of God's presence during which the praying person is open to the inspiration of the Holy Spirit in his or her depth. We use the word 'contemplate' in a non-religious context when we speak about contemplating a sunset or the night sky or when we are moved inwardly by a piece of music. Each is a non-verbal, non-thinking experience which touches us very deeply.

Eastern spiritual writers use the two words 'meditation' and 'contemplation' just the other way about!

But there is a further reason for misunderstanding among

Christians in the West. In our culture, our way of thinking is dualistic: we tend to pair off things with their opposites, for example, contrasting body with soul, the sacred with the secular, the spiritual with the material. In none of the great religions of the world, with the exception of Christianity which has its philosophical roots in the western culture, is there a word for 'religion'. In fact, religion, in our western sense, is not referred to anywhere in the Bible. Most tribal languages in the world have no such word in their vocabulary. It is only found in our western languages because we alone divide life into two compartments, the religious and the profane.

Awareness of this way of thinking is imperative if we are to understand how the word 'meditation' is now used widely in our society no longer as a 'churchy' word. We are now using it in the West with the meaning that it has in the East where it does not have a specific religious connotation.

> 'The yogic meditator, like the Christian meditator, expands to the inexhaustible state of infinite knowledge; his soul or individual consciousness is engulfed by the absolute cosmic consciousness.'
>
> *'Christian Meditation in Light of Yoga'*
> *by Justin O'Brien, D.Th.*
> *in 'Meditation in Christianity'*

There is a further difficulty in translating a word from one language to another, when the translation is from one culture to another. We unhappily use the word 'meditation' for the word in Sanskrit, *dhyana,* as well as for the word *samadhi* one of the eight limbs of Yoga (unity) in which mind transcends discursive thought. The thinker, the thinking process and the thought merge into one reality of supreme consciousness. There simply exists no equivalent word in English.

So when we speak of 'meditation' today we are describing

an exercise which is not purely religious, but is a natural, human technique to enable the mind to reach deeper levels of consciousness, an ancient art that pre-dates all the major religions.

This is what Maharishi himself has to say about one method of meditation which we are especially considering in this book:

> 'The nature of the Transcendental Meditation technique is the spontaneous settling down or refinement of mental activity. It is a method of experiencing the source of thought, the field of pure creative intelligence, in an effortless, systematic manner. Automatically, naturally, and very spontaneously, mental activity becomes refined and eventually the mind settles down to a state of no activity, but with full awareness. The conscious mind gains the state of pure awareness.'

To say that Transcendental Meditation is not religious, is not, however, to preclude the fact that it does have a spiritual dimension. That is to say, the entry into transcendental consciousness brings about a growth in our wholeness: it unifies our body, mind and spirit by putting us in touch with the centre of our being. And the centre of our being is the point at which the Divine touches us. For this reason, people who have started to meditate for purely physical or psychological reasons begin to find, after a time, that they are undergoing a spiritual awakening, maybe even leading to a whole range of spiritual experiences.

> 'No movement in religious life has any value unless it is also a movement inwards to the 'still centre' of your existence, where Christ is.'
>
> *Pope John Paul II at Maynooth, Ireland, October 1st 1979.*

Because of confusion over the word 'meditation', when listening to an introductory talk about this technique, given by a qualified TM teacher, Christians sometimes wonder why no mention is made of its spiritual benefits, but only about the physical, psychological and social advantages to be gained from it. The spiritual advantage is rarely mentioned because since TM is neither a religion nor religious the TM movement which promotes a natural, human technique, does not wish to have itself wrongfully classed with the Sects and Cults.

But spiritual benefit, there certainly is. The enrichment to the areas of mind, body, behaviour and environment, which TM brings about, cannot be separated from — still less be in opposition to — enrichment of the spiritual dimension.

> 'You should bring your reasoning mind to stillness. Understanding of things that cannot be seen belongs to pure consciousness. We speak of pure consciousness when the spirit dwells in the highest truth without any admixture of imaginative thinking. In order to achieve this you must learn to tie down your wandering memories and ideas and thereby silence thinking.'
>
> *Francisco de Osuna*
> *a Spanish Franciscan of the fifteenth century*

Meditation: The Path to Wisdom

Our western world is so science-orientated that we can easily lose sight of the fact that there is more than one way of acquiring knowledge.

The way we know best is what we call rational knowledge: it comes to us through our using our human capacity to reason. Information enters our mind from outside us by way of the five senses (hearing, smelling, seeing, touching, tasting). We then reason about this information — the most obvious is from cause to effect (if I turn on this electric switch, what will be the effect?) or from effect to cause (the milk bottle has been knocked over: it must have been done by the cat). This way of exercising our minds is the method of modern science.

But there is another way of knowing which comes from inside our minds. We call it intuitive knowledge or wisdom. For no explicable cause, and often in the most unlikely moment, we receive a flash of inspiration. It provides us with a form of knowledge, of certainty about something, that we are often not able to put into words. Dictionaries define intuition as 'the quick perception of truth or knowledge without conscious attention or reasoning', 'knowledge from within'.

We receive our knowledge of God — the Divine Mystery — in these two ways too. We learn *about* God through information we receive from outside us: through what our religion teaches us. Thus the Christian learns about God through the pages of the Bible as interpreted for us by the Church.

But there is a difference between knowing *about* God and

knowing *God*. I know about people I have never met because I received my information second-hand. I even believe in their existence because I trust the truthfulness of my informants. On the other hand, I know a person because I have met him or her: I have an experience of the person. This is direct knowledge.

Many Christians today know a lot *about* God because they believe in the words of the Bible and in what the Church teaches them. But how many can say that they actually know God — have had a direct experience of God? While the knowledge *about* God is available only to a person who follows a particular religion, a believer, an *experience* of God (intuitive knowledge from within) is available to any of us by virtue of our nature as human beings.

> 'Since starting TM God has become much more intimate to me. I experience God as being present everywhere and within myself.'
>
> *Hasso Schelp, journalist, Germany.*

However, we need both forms of knowledge — they complement each other. A knowledge about God without an inner experience of God provides only an empty form of religion, a religion of beliefs and observances that touches only our external lives. On the other hand, the direct, intuitive experience of God requires the outer revelation offered by a religion, to give an interpretation of the inner experience.

Meditation is a means of acquiring that inner experience because it enables the mind to transcend thinking and to enter into a deeper state of consciousness in which we can experience the source of all life, the presence of the Divine at the very centre of our being.

This is why so many Christians, when they begin the practice of TM, say that the practice leads them to a new, deeper, more enlightened understanding of the Bible and of Christian beliefs.

'I was no longer practising the Catholic Faith in which I had been brought up, when I started TM. It took me from what had been a mechanical practice of my religion, to a real dialogue with God. I began to see the divine presence in everyone.'

Francoise Tixier, a social counsellor, Paris.

Meditation: A Means to Grow from Unreality to Reality

From our earliest years each of us has been trying to discover his or her true identity. At first unconsciously, and as we grew into adolescence, more consciously, we have been trying to find the answer to the question: Who am I?

Even before we were at an age when we were able to ask the question consciously, we had started to build up a Self which we wished to project. We did this first by imitating people we admired or people close to us. We tried to present an image of ourselves that we wanted people to see, to admire and to love. In so far as the ingredients of this Self came from outside us, were imitations of other people, we were building up a false, unreal Self. The real Self, our true identity, is born from within our own depth.

A Christian would express this by saying that when God created me he had a unique person in mind, like no other among the five billion people presently populating the earth. My life's work is to grow in knowledge of who that person really is and to take the means to become that person, the fully human person, that God intends me to become. In other words, my real Self.

Sadly, all of us spend a great deal of energy trying to give reality to our unreal Self, which is no more than the façade we wish to project, the sham hero we want people to admire, or the suit of armour we defensively wear lest people discover our weak points. And we waste so much of our time with the concerns of that world which stimulates and reinforces our false Self. If we think for a moment about some of our acquaintances we have to say of a few of them: 'After all these years I have never met the real John Blogs. He has only let me meet him at surface level.' The greatest tragedy would be, if at the end of our lives, God has to say: 'I do not recognise you. You are not the person I created you to become.'

The false Self battles to dominate the true Self. It divides us in two: prevents us from being whole. The source of our wholeness, in which body, mind and spirit are in harmony, is the real Self, because the unifying power comes from within the depth of our being. Those brought up in the Christian tradition will have been taught from childhood that God's will for them is that they should be holy. The word 'holy' can send a shiver down the spine of some people. It conjures up pictures of simpering sugary saints. In fact, the word 'holy' comes from the same root as 'whole'. A truly holy person is one who has grown into the real integrated Self whom God intended him or her to be, and inevitably in doing so has grown into a close relationship with God, the source of each person's reality. The real Self is able to acknowledge and accept her faults and weaknesses as much as being able to acknowledge and accept her strengths and gifts. This is true humility: to live as the reality God created us to be.

To become an integrated, real, whole person can take a lifetime — and some never become it this side of death. In the passage of death is the final letting go. Letting go not only of all our possessions, but of all falsehoods, all pretence. That final letting go is less agonising if we have begun it already during life. The process is like peeling off the layers and layers that make up an onion until one comes to the core at the centre.

Meditation is an exercise which helps us in this process. By regularly meditating I am entering into my innermost Self and gradually meeting the real Self at the centre of my being. The more I am able to recognise and accept the real Self, the person I am in my deepest identity, the more I am able to let go of the false unreal Self.

The more we regularly meditate, the more our life is taken over by the real deep Self and the less we are tossed about on the surface of life by the false Self which exists only at the surface level. This is what meditators mean when they say their practice of meditation causes them to live at a deeper level. All their actions become more powerful and effective because they originate from a greater depth within them.

Regular meditation causes us to move into a more real world, or rather, to move about our world while recognising in it a reality that we had not suspected existed. It is like people born completely colour-blind who have grown up knowing only a world of blacks and whites and greys. Suddenly they see everything in full colour. They are seeing the same objects but now recognising that they have a quality they had never suspected.

In this new vision of reality we appreciate the interconnectedness of everything and experience ourselves as part of that.

When we meditate we are coming into contact with our deepest Selves, our real Selves. The more we meditate the more this real Self is enabled to develop and bit by bit replace our false Self. Both in our own Selves and in the outlook and awareness we have of our surroundings we are growing from the unreal to the real. And because we are beginning to act out of reality we release the energies of the unconscious and all sorts of new avenues are open to us which we had never dreamed about before.

Meditation enables us to live at and out of an ever deeper consciousness. The more we allow our real Self to develop, the more facility we gain for living in the conscious presence of the source of all reality: God.

'Late have I loved you, O beauty, so ancient and so new; late have I loved you! For behold you were within me, and I outside; and I sought you outside and in my ugliness fell upon those lovely things that you have made. You were within me and I was not with you.'

Confessions of St. Augustine

Meditation: The Way to Wholeness

One of the characteristics of our times is that the pragmatic, rational, experimental world of the scientist is drawing nearer to the experiential, transcendent world of the mystic. Ever since the birth of modern science in the 17th century the two ways of understanding our world have been along very different paths.

Western science has, until well into the 20th century, offered a very mechanistic world view: that the world and all within it — including our human bodies — are made up of parts. We notice the application of this principle most obviously in the science of medicine. When a part of the body is unwell a medicine is prescribed to cure that particular part, just as when a machine breaks down the faulty part is repaired.

The shift today is towards understanding our world as a living organism and all that goes to make it up — ourselves included — as part of that organism. We form part of a whole where the whole is greater than the sum of its parts. In the medical field doctors are beginning to appreciate that to maintain health it is not enough to cure one ailing part of the body but to take into account the total life of persons, their environment, their relationships, their family medical history and those things in their daily round which cause them stress.

All the great spiritual masters and mystics of East and West have always taught that life is essentially one. Deep within all of us is a desire for wholeness — a God-given desire.

This innate desire is now manifesting itself in our everyday lives in the West. Children are being taught to be co-operative rather than competitive, we take means to eat a better balanced diet, we are more concerned about our relationship with the environment, we feel a responsibility to give aid to the victims of disaster at the other side of the globe because these people share our humanity, we have a growing sense of our all being part of one earth.

This growing awareness, this increasing attraction towards wholeness, is a sign of the level of consciousness which is evolving in humanity today. For Christians this move towards unity should come as no surprise. St. Paul describes God's great design for his creation as a journey towards unity, revealed to us by Jesus: 'In all his wisdom and insight, God did what he had purposed, and made known to us the secret plan he had already decided to complete by means of Christ. This plan, which God will complete when the time is right, is to bring all creation together, everything in heaven and on earth, with Christ as head' (Eph. 1: 8-10).

Transcendental Meditation as a technique has come to us in the West today as a particularly important gift which we can exercise to sharpen our awareness of the source of all life. The practice unfolds higher states of consciousness which causes a change in our perception of things, inviting us to respond accordingly. Our senses become more attuned to the rhythm of the universe and we experience a growing harmony, peace and oneness, within ourselves and all around us.

The transcendence brought about by meditation does not create the wholeness we describe: it is already there but we are largely unaware of its existence. Meditation produces in us an awareness that enables us to experience and comprehend life in its real nature as a whole and as having its source in the Godhead.

For many people the first weeks and months of practising TM bring dramatic experiences because they are discovering this new dimension to their lives. Some have found that their practice of meditation brings about a deeper awareness of and appreciation for the Word of God in the Bible, for the beliefs of their Faith and for the meaning of the Sacraments. A few may even have what they might describe as an experience of mystical phenomena. It is important to recognise that these are happening purely at the psychological level. All spiritual writers say they should be ignored, certainly not encouraged. They may result from a sudden and extreme release of stress. They are no indication of holiness nor are they a measure of our spiritual growth. The great Christian Mystics teach that spiritual growth is a gift of God and develops through a growing relationship with God and an awareness of his presence in our depth. It is not something we can produce by our own effort. We can only open ourselves to God's Spirit acting in our depth.

There is just one way to measure our closeness to God and that is the measure of charity: the degree to which we love God which is expressed by our willingness to do the Will of God and by our love of our neighbour. What we mean in concrete by the expression 'the Will of God' is often a mystery to many. Hans Kung, a well-known German theologian, has described it as that which we wish for ourselves when we want what is the very best for us. Maharishi describes it as living in accordance with natural law. Both are describing a life which is in harmony with God's creative power and evolutionary design for our world.

'For me, TM has been both a 'tranquilliser' and a 'synthesiser'. Being something of a workaholic, it has helped to slow me down, focus my energies and enabled me to live in a more unified and harmonious way.'

Diarmuid O'Murchu, a priest and social psychologist

Transcendental Meditation has a Social Dimension

So far we have considered Transcendental Meditation as being of benefit to the meditator only. The accusing finger is sometimes pointed at the meditator as one who seeks flight from reality: as one who is concerned only with his or her own personal development. Meditating has been called an ego-trip.

While this might be the motivation that attracts a few people to it, the effect it produces is infinitely wider.

There is a social dimension to the practice of TM which operates at two levels. One is at the affective level: metaphorically speaking, it allows the heart to expand. The practice causes us to become more open, more loving, more compassionate because we are gradually becoming more whole. In fact we have a growing experience of entering into, of being one with, the oneness of all humanity. Because it is an experience, this effect is difficult to describe. But it could be said that we increasingly feel that our own essential being is part of the very essence of humanity, so that other people's sadness becomes our own, their joy is our own joy — at a very deep level.

The other social effect is at the scientific level: the influence of Transcendental Meditation on the field of consciousness.

Our great-grandfathers knew nothing about radio waves until an inventor named Marconi demonstrated a way in which a human voice could be sent from one box, the transmitter, to another, the receiver, beyond the natural range of the voice. And there was no connection between the boxes: the transmission was wire-less. Nowadays every household makes use of this discovery without any degree of amazement in its use of radio, television and even satellite dish.

Today we are discovering something further: the effects of waves sent out by the human mind. Our brains are like radio transmitters and receivers and, like these instruments, the more finely the mind can be tuned, by passing into deeper states of consciousness, the greater the potential for having an effect on the surroundings. This phenomenon has been researched in regard to Transcendental Meditation. In TM circles it is given the name 'The Maharishi Effect' because Maharishi predicted it as early as 1960.

It has been observed that when a number of people in a given area regularly practise Transcendental Meditation they influence the field of consciousness in that area in such a way that there is a decrease of stress. Scientific studies made by independent researchers over the last couple of decades in cities throughout the world have discovered that when as few as 1% of the population of these cities practise Transcendental Meditation the decrease in stress becomes manifest in such phenomena as a drop in the number of accidents and traffic fatalities, a lowering of the crime rate, less violence, a fall in the number of hospital admissions.

Furthermore, it has been revealed by these studies that when the advanced Sidhi programme of Transcendental Meditation is practised by a group of people together, producing brain waves of the same frequency, as few as the square root of 1% can influence their environment in this manner. The effect can be compared to that of a platoon of soldiers marching over a suspension bridge. Thirty separate individuals crossing the bridge will have no special effect on the bridge, but the same number of soldiers marching across in step will cause the bridge to start swinging. The physical effect of the rhythm they produce when in step is far greater than that of their total foot power.

A group of meditators is releasing into the population's nervous system the creative energy and purification needed to throw off the inhibiting effects of self-centredness, of the

Since January 1987 Transcendental Meditation has been introduced to prisoners (11,000) and staff (900) in 31 prisons in the West African country of Senegal. The effects have been dramatic. As listed by Col. Mamadou Diop, Director of Penitentiary Administration, these are:

Prisoners:

* Immediate improvement in sleep — less insomnia,
* Very sharp reduction in irritability and aggressiveness,
* More confidence in themselves and in the future,
* Improvement in relationships between prisoners,
* Reduction in the number of thefts,
* Improvement in health,
* Marked decrease in drug-taking.

Staff:

* More concern for the prisoners,
* More self-control,
* Greater conscientiousness,
* Better health,
* Less absenteeism and lateness.

Prison as a whole:

* Almost complete cessation of fights between prisoners,
* Marked decrease in rule violations,
* Decrease in the number of attempted escapes,
* Sharp decrease in the number of medical consultations.

In Senegal, before the introduction of TM, some 90% of prisoners released after serving their sentence could have been expected to return to prison within one month. However, six months after an amnesty in June 1988 when 2,390 prisoners were released, only 200 were back in prison again and of these 80% were non-meditators.

unreal Self. Greater tenderness, love and understanding, sensitivity and awareness, forgiveness and generosity — all of which are social virtues — then follow naturally for the benefit, not only of the meditators, but for all around. TM teachers explain this in terms of reduced negativity and stress in the collective consciousness.

In this respect the Christian who practises Transcendental Meditation is enabled to fulfil the mission of a follower of Christ: to manifest the existence of, and make a reality in this world, God's Kingdom of justice, love and peace.

Meditation in the Life of Jesus

Nowhere in the Bible do we find any instructions as to how to meditate. But is it right to presume from that fact that meditation in some form or other was not practised by Jesus? And if it is not mentioned specifically that Jesus meditated are we right in concluding from that, as some Christians do, that therefore a practice like Transcendental Meditation should not be practised by Christians?

Most of what we know about the day-to-day life of Jesus comes to us from the four Gospels. However, that said, we must understand that the Gospels were not diaries of his life nor even biographies — and certainly have no intention of including everything about him — but were partial accounts of his teaching and actions written many years later and in order to put across a particular message to a particular readership.

At the very end of his Gospel St John writes: 'There are many other things that Jesus did. If they were all written down one by one, I suppose that the whole world could not contain the books that would have to be written'.

So to learn about something not specifically stated we have to examine what we know from the Gospels as a whole. What can we glean about his own meditative practice and what did he teach?

The language Jesus spoke was Aramaic: it was the language of his followers and of the crowds of people he addressed. In fact it was the common spoken language of the Middle East in his time.

Today increasing numbers of middle-eastern biblical scholars believe that the Gospels were originally written in Aramaic — or, if not all of them, at least the Gospel of Matthew.

Why this is important is because Aramaic texts, which would be much closer to the thought forms of Jesus than our Greek version, reveal a depth of mysticism in the sayings of Jesus that is not noticeable in our western translations. The Aramaic texts present a more holistic view of the cosmos, making less distinction, for example, between 'body', 'mind' and 'spirit' than the Greek text does. Neil Douglas-Klotz, an Aramaic scholar, writes: '"Heaven" in Aramaic ceases to be a metaphysical concept and presents the image of light and sound shining through all creation'.

Jesus the Meditator

Besides his faithfulness to the religious practices required of Jews at the time — weekly prayer in the synagogue, occasional visits to the Temple in Jerusalem, fasts, religious observances in the home — we know that he liked to retire on his own into the hills and would 'pass the whole night in prayer'. Six such occasions are mentioned, but there must have been many more.

Do we know of there being any meditative tradition among the Jews of Jesus' time? The Talmud (a compilation of comments on Jewish religious law dating from a few hundred years after Jesus) talking about the modes of prayer of the wise, mentions that they would start their period of prayer with one hour of silence. (The verb used was *shohim,* which has the connotation of 'waiting' and 'being').

We cannot overlook the possibility that Jesus learnt some form of eastern meditation during those 'hidden' years which preceded his three years of preaching. After all, Palestine was on the trade route from East to West and we notice that a number of his parables have their parallel in early eastern literature.

More revealing, is the effect on him of a life of meditation: he was clearly an enlightened person. We notice his complete non-attachment, his single-mindedness in pursuing the mission he believed God had given him, his selfless love and service, his keen mind, his equanimity when challenged, his fearlessness and deep peace. These, in fact, are the characteristics of enlightenment that we find mentioned by the sages of all cultures and traditions, and that we can read about in, for instance, the *Tao Te Ching*, the *Gita*, and the *Hadith*. Then there were the special powers he was able to exercise: multiplication of material objects, power over storms, walking on water, physical and spiritual healing.

We Christians become so used to thinking of Jesus as divine that we can easily eclipse the fact that he was fully human. His enlightenment and his unusual powers came to him, not because he was God, but because he was a fully developed human person. If we are called to follow Jesus it is because each of us is invited, as St. Paul puts it, 'to become mature people, reaching to the very height of Christ's full stature' (Eph. 4:13).

In the second century after Jesus, St. Irenaeus wrote: 'Our Lord Jesus Christ did through his transcendent love become what we are, that we might become what he is'. And two centuries later this was echoed by St. Athanasius, a Bishop and great Christian scholar: 'He was made man that we might be made God'. These early Christians understood, perhaps more clearly than we, the fantastic fact that potentially we can also become divine. It was Jesus himself who said: 'I have come in order that you may have life — life in all its fullness' (John 10:10) as well as: 'Whoever believes in me will do what I do — yes, he will do even greater things' (John 14:12).

Jesus' Teaching

Nowhere in the four Gospels is it mentioned that Jesus taught a technique of meditation. But we cannot conclude from this that he did not. He certainly spoke a lot about the inner life and the importance of developing it.

What we notice is that he offered people the teaching that they were ready to hear and able to accept. To the general public he gave basic ethical norms to enable them to live more in accordance with God's design for humanity (which he referred to as God's Kingdom). So he mostly employed parables (Matt. 13:34) which each listener was able to comprehend at their own level of consciousness. To a chosen few, his disciples, he imparted a higher teaching. 'The knowledge of the secrets of the Kingdom of God has been given to you, but to the rest it comes by means of parables' (Luke 8:10). Mark writes: 'He spoke the word to them (the crowd) as far as they were capable of understanding it... but he explained everything to his disciples when they were alone' (4:33-34). Among the Apostles, Peter, James and John were given more advanced teaching and allowed a mystical experience on Mount Tabor: the event we call the Transfiguration (Matt. 17:1-9). Jesus even said he would not 'give to dogs what is holy or throw (his) pearls before swine' (Matt. 7:6).

Since the Gospel writers and St. Paul wrote for the general public their writings do not include the private instructions the disciples received. As the young Church grew she created a single code of doctrine that was meant for the masses. Thus the Church's ethics, ritual and dogma have become identified as those of Jesus, and we can be forgiven for thinking that he never taught the higher spiritual path.

But we notice that the opening words of Jesus' preaching as recorded in St. Mark's Gospel (1:15) are: 'The time has come and the Kingdom of God is close at hand. Repent, and believe the Good News'. The word 'repent' is one translation of the Greek word *metanoia,* (the Gospel texts on which our translations are based were written in Greek) and is often taken to mean 'express sorrow', 'feel guilty', 'do penance'. Literally translated *metanoia* means 'change your mind'. Here Jesus is using the expression at a deeper level than we use it in everyday conversation, meaning 'change your decision'. He means change your mind-set, change your attitudes, your paradigm, change your level of consciousness. In fact, the word means 'to go beyond the mind' (just as 'metaphysics' means to go beyond physics) which we might interpret as to transcend. This is born out by Jesus saying to the Jewish leader Nicodemus: 'No one can see the Kingdom of God unless he is born again' (John 3:3). The change of consciousness has to be as radical as that: live in an entirely new dimension. Only in this way will we become Kingdom people, able to live heaven on earth.

Meditation: A Means of Growth for Christians

The title is not meant to suggest that Transcendental Meditation is particularly for Christians rather than for anyone else. We have already said that it is a natural, human exercise, not a religious devotion. But there are a number of pre-conceived ideas about meditation — in the non-religious sense that we described earlier — that cause hesitation or even suspicion in the minds of some Christians. We will look at four of these before we consider the positive reasons for recommending the practice.

First, an unease is sometimes expressed because the technique for meditating offered us today comes from an eastern and not a western, nor a Biblical, source. We forget that an enormous amount of assimilation has always gone on between cultures — never more so than today with our ease of world-wide communication. The Middle-East — the cradle of Christianity — has always been a crossing point of trade routes between East and West, between North and South, which facilitated the passage of ideas. Some of the texts we find in the Bible are taken from 'pagan' sources but put to use to describe a theological truth. St. Paul's oft-quoted phrase 'In him we live and move and have our being' (Acts 17:28) comes from a secular source, thought by some authors to be the 6th century BC poet Epimenides. Some passages in the Old Testament are identical with those of the Upanishads.

It is almost certain that there were Hindu and Buddhist monks in Alexandria (Egypt) in the first and second centuries AD. They must surely have influenced the young Christian communities there.

> 'Much of Christian mysticism was informed by the East, and much of Irish Christianity has its direct origins in the Vedic tradition. I believe, far from creating discontinuities with my own origins, Transcendental Meditation has greatly added to my theological understanding of them, and enriched for me their possibilities'.
>
> *Rev. Sean O'Conchuir S.J.*
> *An Irish Jesuit Priest*

We can hardly do better than follow St. Paul's advice to the new Christians in Thessalonica: 'Do not restrain the Holy Spirit; do not despise inspired messages. Put all things to the test: keep what is good and avoid every kind of evil' (I Thess. 5:19-22).

A second hesitation arises from the relation of TM to prayer. (We will discuss this in the next chapter.) How can an exercise which is not in itself a form of prayer contribute to our spiritual growth? The question only arises if we separate what is spiritual from what is mental or physical in our lives. If we have a holistic understanding of life then we will appreciate that anything we do — physical exercises, study, etc. — which develops our human potential also has a spiritual value because it is contributing to our becoming the fully human person God created us to be.

A third reason for fear of the practice of TM that some Christians express is that it will cause them to empty their minds, and then there is the danger that evil spirits will take possession of them.

In the practice of TM you do not empty the mind. In fact it is impossible for the mind to stop thinking. It is the mind's nature to think as it is the heart's nature to pump blood. What happens is that during the practice of Transcendental Meditation thoughts gradually become finer, less clear-cut, more subtle and peaceful and because the use of the mantra refines the activity of the mind a sense of calmness and oneness is experienced. No spirits, evil or good, can take possession of your mind without your permitting it.

At no time, though, do you lose control; you continue to be aware of external noises and you can stop meditating the moment you wish. So there is no danger of someone else taking possession of the mind. It is in no way like hypnosis or spiritualism.

'In the earnest exercise of mystical contemplation, you leave the senses and the operations of reason and all things that the senses of reason can perceive, to the end that you raise yourself by this unknowing to union with Him who is above all being and all knowledge; that is, to raise yourself by absolute detachment from yourself and all things, stripped of everything and free from every hindrance to that stream of divine brightness coming forth from this inner obscurity.'

These words were written in the fifth or sixth century by a monk in Syria who wrote under the title of Dionysius the Areopagite. His works were translated into Latin in the seventh century and were greatly respected in the Christian Church in the West, being cited by theologians and mystics as a spiritual authority. His writings are actually influenced by Indian metaphysics.

A fourth reason for hesitation in the minds of some lay Christians is that for centuries, in the western world, meditation and contemplation have been regarded as the prerogative of monks and nuns, those who 'left the world' by living in monasteries and convents. Indeed, their detachment from the daily concerns of normal life, their fasts, penances and other ascetic practices were regarded as a condition for entering into the higher states of consciousness which spiritual writers referred to as mysticism.

We ordinary mortals just did not have a chance. We were simply told to 'say our prayers'. Strange really, when one considers that these same spiritual writers assured us that the eternal destiny of us all after death would be a state of unity and God consciousness — or 'contemplation of God', as they expressed it. If it is truly to be our joy then, would we not be encouraged to journey in the right direction by being allowed a foretaste already now?

Only in our own day, under the influence, as we all are, of a developing global consciousness, are we growing in awareness that the possibility of entering higher states of consciousness is a natural process for human nature and not the preserve of the few who are called 'Contemplatives'.

But more than that, the New Era of Consciousness is itself a product of a new stage in human evolution. The big steps in the development of our universe so far have been from matter to plant life to animal life to intelligent human life. This new step, the beginnings of which we are witnessing in our own lifetime, is a breakthrough which is no longer physical but psychic — the evolution of the human mind. This can be hastened by more and more people beginning to develop their God-given mental faculties — 90% of which lie dormant — by transcending the commonly experienced states of consciousness (deep sleep, dreaming and wakefulness) and enjoying higher states from which can be drawn new powers and faculties. We are entering the Age of Transcendence. This Age is characterised by among other things, the search for wholeness, inner peace and happiness and for a sense of fulfilment in life. This is pursued by some within, by others outside, a religious context. Meditation is increasingly being considered the chief means to achieve this goal.

Fortunately an increasing number of people in the institutional Church are beginning to realise that any exercise, no matter what its origin, which enables a person to live a more fully human life is at the same time going to enable them tolive more fully as Christians.

> 'Christians have sometimes asked me about the relevance of TM (and other forms of meditation) for their faith; and I have answered that whatever develops human potential should also develop Christian faith, provided this faith is alive and nourished by scripture and liturgy. I mean that if human potential is enhanced, then the totality of one's commitment to Christ can also be deepened.
>
> *Fr. William Johnston, a Jesuit, in 'Silent Music'*

Because meditation is a holistic exercise — benefiting the whole person, physically, mentally and spiritually — its fruits are those of the Holy Spirit: love, joy, peace, patience, kindness, goodness, faithfulness, gentleness and self-control, as listed by St. Paul (Col. 5:22). Hundreds of scientific research studies, as well as the experience of millions of people around the world — of all faiths, cultures and races — have verified that these are precisely the results which flow from Transcendental Meditation.

Increasingly, more Christians today are sensing that there should be more to their religious life than church-going, than good works and charitable actions. The missing dimension is the 'soul' of religious life — that which gives it meaning. Religion can easily become simply a faithfulness to external practices. It had become so for the Jews in the time of Jesus and he was continually pointing out to them that without the inner dimension they had lost the true meaning of religion. This is what theologians mean today when they say that Jesus came to liberate us from religion: from a purely external practice, as if we could win God's favour by our good deeds, by observing the law meticulously. Jesus said to his fellow Jews that in future true worshippers would worship God 'in spirit and in truth' (John 4:23).

Since the 1960s many clergy, nuns and even some Bishops have learnt and practised TM. It is taught in monasteries, convents and seminaries, to everyone's great spiritual benefit.

Transcendental Meditation and Prayer

We have already said that Transcendental Meditation as practised in the East is a natural, human exercise for the development of greater consciousness and not, as the word 'meditation' is used in western Christian circles, a form of prayer. Must we then say that it has no relationship to what Christians mean by prayer?

Put simply, what Christians regard as prayer is conscious communication with God. This means much more than speaking to God, asking God to supply our needs, or even giving praise to God as we do in public worship. There is a much deeper level of prayer than this: it is to be aware that we live in the presence of God, that God is present at the very centre of our being. This more profound form of prayer — which in the Christian vocabulary is referred to as contemplation — has been called by the mystics the prayer of quiet: a form of silent prayerfulness in which no words are needed, but nevertheless being actively attentive to God's presence in the depth of our being. It is not unlike the wordless communication that takes place between a mother and her baby in which they both gaze at each other in silence and in love. In prayer, the divine presence we are aware of with love is at the still point of our existence. The Transcendental Meditation technique enables the mind to contact this deepest centre of our being. If that journey is made by a person who believes that it is God who is found and is active at that deepest centre, then his or her meditation is indeed prayer, the very purest form of prayer. As William Johnston, a Jesuit, says in his book on meditation, *Silent Music*, 'What makes meditation religious or non-religious is one's sense of values and one's motivation'. In other words, what makes a Christian's practice of Transcendental Meditation a form of prayer is to have the desire to enter the deepest form of communication with God. This desire does not have to be consciously expressed each time one begins the meditation exercise. In fact, it might be better if it is not. Trying to adopt this or that attitude towards one's TM practice may interfere with the innocence, and therefore with the naturalness and the effectiveness of the technique. What is required is an overall orientation of the mind towards God: what spiritual writers call our 'fundamental option', or choice, for God.

> 'The Christian who takes up TM, if his vision and motivation are enlivened by his faith, realises by this faith that he is entering upon a way of very pure prayer. He is leaving all behind, all his thoughts, feelings, desires, in order to enter into God. Even if in a particular instance he does not actually transcend and enter into the fourth state of consciousness, his motivation, his outreach towards God is still there as a very restful and beautiful state of contemplation, of contemplative union with God.'
>
> *Cistercian monk, Basil Pennington, in his book 'Daily we Touch Him'.*

Our fundamental option for God determines the religious or non-religious value of *anything* we do, not just TM. Our taking food, our work, recreation, relationships — any of these can be an act of devotion to God, depending on our attitude.

Our attitude, in turn, depends on our state of consciousness. (By 'attitude' is not meant a 'mood', but rather a spontaneous, natural way in which one approaches something.) As consciousness develops, our attitudes change. With Transcendental Meditation, consciousness expands and attitudes spontaneously become more life-supporting, more evolutionary.

Since TM develops consciousness, with time, this makes people more religious, spontaneously. Time and time again, people who have started TM who had had, initially, no religious background, no religious inclination, start feeling attracted to their own traditions and start feeling that their meditation is, indeed, something that brings them closer to God. This, incidentally, is another reason why TM is not taught in the context of any religion. TM gives the experience, and people find that spontaneously they become more religious, whatever religion they belong to.

In the Jewish Scriptures — what we Christians refer to as the Old Testament — we find several references to a silent, aware form of prayer. For instance:

Be silent before the Lord and wait patiently for him. (Ps. 37:7)

Be still and know that I am God. (Ps. 46:10)

The day of the Lord is near, the day when God will act; so be silent in his presence. (Zeph. 1:17)

It is sometimes objected by those Christians who are suspicious of any practice of meditation brought to us from the East, that where the technique consists of the repetition of a mantra taken from the Vedic Scriptures, as in Transcendental Meditation, that these mantras are the names of Hindu gods and that one is thereby unwittingly praying to Hindu gods. They are not, in fact, the names of Hindu gods. They are sounds derived from the Vedic tradition which are suitable for the process of transcending.

Such an objection reveals a fundamental misunderstanding of the nature of prayer. Prayer is an act of the will, so one cannot pray to God (or gods) without intending to, out of ignorance, so to speak. A pygmy wandering about in the Ituri Forest in central Africa reciting the name Jesus without any understanding of its meaning, is neither praying nor calling upon the power of Jesus.

It is sometimes mistakenly thought that Transcendental Meditation consists of the recitation of the mantra. It does not. The mantra is used as a tool to enable the mind to settle down. Eventually, when one experiences transcendental consciousness, the mantra disappears from the mind, much in the same way that one descends from a vehicle upon arriving at the destination. The Vedic mantra used in Transcendental Meditation is only a sound which has no meaning associated with it. We know that every sound produces some sort of effect on the mind, beneficial or otherwise. The sound of a finger nail scratched on a blackboard produces a shudder down the spine: the sound of a flute is uplifting and soothing. The finer or more abstract the level of any vibration, the more powerful its influence. Thus the ancient Vedic scholars chose only those sounds as mantras which would be wholly beneficial to the individual and the environment throughout the whole process of transcending. The mantra is no more than the means to enable the mind to transcend the thinking process, for one to experience the state of complete inner stillness — transcendental consciousness.

'Before ever I started TM, meditation was something of a serious quest for me. Mornings I would spend up to two hours at it. At the end of that time, I would have been round about where I am now after one or two minutes of TM. You can judge for yourself from that what an immense blessing the simple technique has been and how grateful I feel.'

Rev. Sean O'Conchuir S.J.

Meditation: A Key to the Kingdom of Heaven

The core of Jesus' message during the all-too-short three years in which he went public was not, as is often thought, about a new religion — which today we call Christianity — but about a new way of living. It was no accident that his disciples, in their earliest days, were known as the followers of *The Way*. He introduced a new value system. It is summed up in his Sermon on the Mount as the eight 'Be-attitudes'.

He called this new age that he was ushering in 'The Kingdom of Heaven', a phrase that has little impact today except in Church circles but which meant a great deal to his fellow Jews who were his audience.

The kernel of his Kingdom teaching, proposing a new way of living, is all about relationships. What he said about relationships, about society, about the exercise of authority, about the value of even the most lowly person, was so revolutionary that it led to his being executed as a disturber of the peace. He proposed that men and women should have a personal, individual relationship with God, so intimate that God should be understood and related to as the loving Father of each one. In today's scientific jargon we would say this was a religious paradigm shift. Till then the God of his hearers had been understood to be a tribal God with whom the Jewish race, considering themselves as a Chosen People, had made a Covenant. So awesome was their God that his name could not be spoken aloud.

What Jesus did was to raise human beings to a new awareness of their relationship with the Divine and, as a logical consequence, to a new level of relationship with each other. How can I and my neighbours accept that God is our intimate Father, without accepting the demand to relate to each other as closely as brothers and sisters?

St. Paul recognised Jesus' presence in the world as taking humanity a great leap forward: an evolutionary leap, we would say today, towards our final destiny to be united with the Godhead. 'God's plan is to make known his secret to his people, this rich and glorious secret which he has for all peoples. And the secret is that Christ is in you. For the full content of divine nature lives in Christ, in his humanity, and you have been given full life in union with him.' (Col. 1:27, 2:9-10).

Not only was the Jesus event a great leap forward for humanity, but it was a well-timed one. For thousands of years the human mind had been progressively deepening what today we would call its religious life and understanding of matters spiritual. Over the two thousand years previous to the birth of Jesus, the Jewish people were undergoing a process of refining their understanding of God — moving from the notion of many gods to the idea of their god being the superior god to an understanding that there is only one God — till such time that they were ready for the next step in this unfolding of the divine mystery by Jesus. We might ask: today two thousand years on, how many of us are sufficiently mature to be able to accept wholeheartedly the message of Jesus in full? Very few. Humanity is still not sufficiently spiritually evolved.

What is apparent in the Bible is the acknowledgment that humanity is on a journey. There is a beginning and an end, not only to humanity but to the whole cosmos. I have already quoted the following words of St. Paul in a previous chapter but it is good to read them again in this context and from a different translation. 'Such is the richness of the grace which God has showered on us in all wisdom and insight. He has let us know the mystery of his purpose, the hidden plan he so kindly made in Christ from the beginning to act upon when the times had run their course to the end: that he would bring everything together under Christ, as head, everything in the heavens and everything on earth.' (Eph.1:8-10).

Scientists have marked out the stages of this journey from the initial Big Bang. Very few theologians today would not agree that the journey has been made by evolutionary steps. While scientists are able to tell us *when* and *how* creation began and to define the stages of its development, they cannot tell us *why*. That is the field of theologians. For centuries the studies of scientists and theologians have been running along parallel paths, each suspicious of each other. But the second half of this century has seen a remarkable meeting of minds on the part of both — for a variety of reasons which we cannot develop here — so that their respective paths are now drawing closer, each acknowledging that they are studying the same phenomena, albeit from different perspectives.

> 'Contemporary developments in science challenge theology far more deeply than did the introduction of Aristotle into Western Europe in the thirteenth century. Yet these developments also offer to theology a potentially important resource. Just as Aristotelian philosophy, through the ministry of such great scholars as St. Thomas Aquinas, ultimately came to shape some of the most profound expressions of theological doctrine, so can we not hope that the sciences of today, along with all forms of human knowing, may invigorate and inform those parts of the theological enterprise that bear on the relation of nature, humanity and God?'
>
> *Pope John Paul II in a message to the Director of the Vatican Observatory. 1st June 1988.*

One of the elements that has caused this convergence is a new understanding of the world. While theologians were coming to appreciate that God's action could only be understood in the context of his whole creation, and not as isolated from or parallel to it, scientists were coming to realise that the visible world could only be understood when considered in relation to the observer and not as a distinct object apart from ourselves. Until half a century ago 'the world' was regarded by theologians as 'fallen', the realm of sin, and the task of the pastor was to raise people to a spiritual life above the world — through Church membership, of course.

The background to this was the belief in two layers, as it were, to God's creation — two parallel histories. The one was secular history, tainted with sinfulness, the other salvation history in which God was rescuing fallen creatures and leading them to their salvation....in heaven, after death.

The theological shift that has taken place is in understanding that there is only one world upon which, within which, God is active bringing about his design. God's plan — his Kingdom — is for the whole universe and unfolds nowhere else than in creation's entirety. It follows that great leaps in creation's evolution are also great leaps in God's plan. Until now these great leaps have been of the biological order — from matter to plant life to animal life to intelligent human life — and have taken hundreds of millions of years to progress, although each subsequent step has followed the previous one in a shorter interval of time. Change is as old as time, but it has never been constant: it is always accelerating.

Nowhere is this more evident than in human history. To pass from hunter to farmer took some 1,900,000 years, from farmer to industrialist some 101,700 years, from industrialist to our present information age a mere 300 years. And now in this information age accelerated change is even more evident in the new technologies that confront us each day. Where next? And when?

We have already mentioned some of the signs around us that reveal that we are embarked upon the next great evolutionary leap for humanity, but unlike previous leaps which were biological and happened automatically, unwilled and unplanned, this is an evolution of the human mind and so comes about only if and when we will it. We can call it a cultural evolution because it will inform the way we live together and the way we relate to our surroundings.

God makes use of our human situations and our creativeness to bring about his design. He used the historical event of the escape of the Israelites from the tyranny of the Pharaohs in Egypt to teach them a lesson about God as their liberator, an image which has coloured all the subsequent history of Jews, Christians and Moslems. If human beings had not invented a way of making wine from grapes and of grinding the seed of corn and cooking the resulting flour on (discovered) fire, there would have been no Last Supper and no Eucharist in our time. With the invention of the printing press the Word of God, in the pages of the Bible, became accessible to millions of people for their personal spiritual nourishment.

If we have discovered in recent years — or rather, rediscovered — techniques of meditation to enable us to enter transcendental consciousness, this too may be seen as a natural development which God is using to move the divine plan further towards its fulfilment by means of this new evolutionary step.

St. Thomas Aquinas, a theological colossus of the Middle Ages, stated that Grace builds on Nature. Grace can be effective only when and as much as our humanity facilitates its operation.

God's plan for his creation is already fulfilled in the Eternal Now of the Godhead but it is still to be worked out in the dimension of time. It is sometimes said that the world as we know it will reach its fulfilment at the end of time. It is more correct to say that the end of time will come about when the world has reached its fulfilment — when heaven will be a reality on earth. It will be a new and unimaginable reality. Not the earth as we know it now but, in the words of the Book of Revelation, 'a new heaven and a new earth'. Jesus was not in a world of fantasy when he taught us to pray: 'thy kingdom come, thy will be done on earth as it is in heaven'. At what point this becomes a reality in our time scale depends upon our capacity and will to co-operate with the eternal plan.

But we suffer from a severe handicap. While change in the material world (things extraneous to us) is happening at an accelerating pace, our psychic world (our innermost selves) takes much longer to adapt to change and is suffering from the pressures of external change with ever increasing human stress. Not only is this caused by trying to squeeze more and more activity into less and less time — we have become human doers rather than human beings — but our spiritual development, the development of our values and attitudes, has not kept pace with our creativity. For all our civilisation and technological progress there is as much cruelty, jealousy, aggression, greed, self-centredness in humanity as there was when human behaviour was first recorded in the Bible two and a half thousand years ago.

Ever since the human being developed the ability to choose, the bottom line of all human endeavours has been for happiness. Right up to our own time this has mostly been looked for in having: having things, having control, having power, having security, having a good reputation. We are human havers, not human beings.

With the present dawn of a new consciousness more people are turning towards their inner being and less to the exterior to provide their happiness. For a growing number of people the preference is for quality rather than for quantity in life. Sociologists tell us of the rise in the number of inner-motivated people in western society today such that it is beginning to overtake the number of outer-motivated people.

The gift of a meditation technique, such as Transcendental Meditation, has come to us just at the moment in our history when humanity needs it most: a technique to enable the inner life to develop, to provide a path to a greater awareness, a means to deepen our relationships with others and with the cosmos, a tool with which to handle stress, a method to awaken the mind to the presence of the Divine in creation and within our innermost being.

Meditation can become the key to the great breakthrough to our next stage of evolution, another step towards the fulfilment of God's eternal plan for his creation: the realisation of the Kingdom in our midst, heaven on earth.

It is now more than 20 years since I learned Transcendental Meditation. My own spiritual journey has led me to Anglican priesthood, and I am now a team vicar, working in a large parish in South-West London. I can thoroughly recommend TM to all Christians who are seeking the deeper meanings of their faith.

A reclamation of the Scriptures, an enhanced understanding of Christ, and an experience of the Holy Spirit of God can now be achieved simply and effortlessly through the regular practice of TM, in the normal course of our regular practice of Christian living.

The time is now right to expand our understanding of the beneficial effects of TM for the future of Christianity.

Revd. John Ansell
Anglican Vicar

Appendix

Useful Addresses

You can be put in touch with a local TM teacher by writing to:

Transcendental Meditation
FREEPOST
London SW1P 4YY

or by telephoning 0800 269303 free of charge.

In 1980, following a week-long Seminar in England for Christians who practise TM, the Christian TM Group was founded in Britain, to be followed by similar groups starting in France and Germany. In America there is an 'Association of Religious Leaders and Scholars Practising TM'. The Group in Britain meets over a weekend twice a year and has as its purpose, in the words of its Constitution:

— to promote a clearer understanding of TM among Christians generally;
— to enable members to appreciate more deeply the help their TM practice gives them in living a fuller Christian life;
— to encourage the relationship between the Christian Church and the TM movement.

Contact can be made with the group by writing to the Membership Secretary:

Miss Angela Pickering
11 Kenilworth Road
Cubbington
LEAMINGTON SPA
CV32 7TN

Suggestions for Further Reading

Adrian B. Smith, (Ed.) *TM: An Aid to Christian Growth.* McCrimmon Publishing Co. Ltd. (paperback, 142pp) A collection of papers by priests and TM teachers, all with the personal experience of practising the TM technique, delivered at a conference of the Christian TM Group.

Maharishi Mahesh Yogi, *The Science of Being and the Art of Living.* (paperback, 320pp) The first detailed description of the philosophy of TM by the person who introduced this ancient practice to the West.

Deepak Chopra MD, *Quantum Healing.* Bantam Books, (paperback and hardback, 278pp) A most readable book, exploring the frontiers of mind/body medicine, by a medical doctor who shows the value of TM to good health.

Orme-Johnson and Wallace, *Scientific Research on the Transcendental Meditation and TM Sidhi programme.* MERU Press. In four volumes (approx. 750pp each) containing over 400 original scientific research papers. Alternatively, a summary booklet of 73pp, MIU Press.

Robert M. Oates, *Creating Heaven on Earth.* MIU Press. (paperback 191pp). The ordinary reader's introduction to the scientific proofs that meditators have a beneficial effect on their environment.

Denise Denniston, *The TM Book, How to enjoy the rest of your life.* Fairfield Press, USA. (paperback, 312pp) Probably the world's most popular introduction to TM, illustrated with cartoons.

New Horizons in Criminology and Penitentiary Science. MERU Press (Paperback, 200pp) A review of the introduction of TM in Senegalese prisons.

J. Anderson and B. Stevens, *Feel Great with TM!,* Golden Arrow Publications (paperback, 80pp) A simple introduction to the benefits of TM with testimonies from a great variety of people who practise the technique.

All the above books are available from Roydon Hall Publications, Roydon Hall, Seven Mile Lane, East Peckham, Tonbridge, Kent. TN12 5NH.

Other books by Adrian B. Smith

A Reason for Hope: The Human Experience of the Kingdom of God. (paperback, 112pp) The author believes that with the new age of consciousness the Kingdom announcement of Jesus is breaking through once more with its original vitality. It is a message of hope with much to tell us of the direction our world is taking.

God and the Aquarian Age: The New Era of the Kingdom. (paperback, 134pp) The author reads the 'signs of the times' and interprets them in the light of God's unfolding plan for his creation. He suggests that our entry into the next millennium will see the birth of a new era of Christianity: the Age of the outpouring of the Spirit.

Both the above are obtainable from bookshops or direct from the publisher: McCrimmon Publishing Co. Ltd., 10 High Street, Great Wakering, Essex. SS3 0EQ.